MY Love Story in Yours

From a teenage grieving heart to rhythms of retreat and rest

Shaunelle Harris Drake

Scripture quotations are taken from The Holy Bible, New International Version® NIV® Copyright © 1973, 1978, 1984, 2011 by Biblica, Inc. Used with permission. All rights reserved worldwide.

Other Scripture quotations (as indicated) are taken from the New King James Version®. Copyright © 1982 by Thomas Nelson. Used by permission. All rights reserved.

www.sitawhile.org

Publisher's Note: This is a work of non-fiction.

Illustrations
Marie Lavis marielavis.com

MY Love Story in Yours/Shaunelle Harris Drake - 1st edition
ISBN 979-8-3347-6286-2 Hardcover
ISBN 979-8-3347-5927-5 Paperback

Jean Harris

Mummy, this is in honour of your memory. You were right, God has taken care of all of us.

To teenagers dealing with loss from death, separation or relocation. I feel your pain. There is hope.

I pen this book for You, my Heavenly Father, because I love You.

CONTENTS

Foreword

Our family retired to bed as usual late on a November Tuesday night, not knowing that by the next morning I would have lost my wife Jean of eighteen years, and that our four children, two in their early teens and two under ten, would have seen their mother alive for the last time.

Completely perplexed and struggling to understand what just hit us, it would be an understatement to say that our world was turned upside down. Instead of looking forward to a work-related relocation to another country within ten days as scheduled, our thoughts turned to more existential issues, including planning a funeral. This was only a few days after burying my own father, the children's grandfather.

It was in this setting that Shaunelle, gradually and unconsciously I believe, began to assume a role, not just as "big sister" but clearly, by instinct, as a mom to her siblings. We were all on our individual journeys of healing in a strange country, away from the logistic and emotional support of family and friends normally available in such circumstances.

As a "rookie" widower, it took me a while to realize that we all experience hurt differently, and we heal differently, based on our roles in the family structure, be it son, daughter, father or husband, and that we recover at different paces. Even as I went through my own struggles, I would periodically wonder how each child was really coping emotionally and, over time, I came to realize that Shaunelle's healing would not be a sprint or even a middle-distance event.

Shaunelle is my eldest, and I read through her memoir with moist eyes, as she describes what happened that November morning when Jean died. I reflected on what it would have meant to her, and that it marked the beginning of her own journey through grief, as a teenager, and into adulthood. What struck me was that, although her journey to healing has been a long one, she did not remain stuck at any stage of the process – she had been open to opportunities for healing along the way.

Shaunelle shares her story with others on a similar journey of pain, grief and healing. This book offers a pathway of hope for teenagers and others, to process their own grief arising from traumatic events, like the loss of a parent or loved one.

Now, more than three decades later, Shaunelle's memoir reminds me of the value of pausing to take stock and reflect on the past with thanksgiving; As she puts it: 'remembering to remember.' This is one of the many ways that our Heavenly Father has been answering my prayer, expressed in the words of the closing hymn at Jean's funeral, 'Guide me, O Thou Great Jehovah, Pilgrim through this barren land…. hold me with Thy powerful hand.'

Leon Harris (Shaunelle's Daddy)

Introduction

When you wake up in the wee hours of the morning and in the quietness of the moment you suddenly hear a voice say, "My story is in yours", you perk up and listen.

My heart responded with curiosity, "Huh, what?"

While trying to preserve the calm and stillness of the morning, I lay in bed and continued listening. Was this God speaking to me?

I kept the dialogue going in my heart, and soon realized this was indeed a sacred moment. It came with a prompt to do some writing, once again. Yet, this time there was a sense of urgency because when I asked, "So do I literally get up and do it now?", the answer back to me was, "Well, if not now, when?" It was October 19, 2023.

MY Love Story in Yours is the red contrast dye running through your life giving you clues to uncover your Heavenly Father's love.

I am amazed at the power of distance, to give a different perspective. The beauty of a waterfall from afar shifts to utter awe and wonder when you stand next to its mighty rushing waters. Admiring a well-formed forest pattern from the window seat of an airplane feels quite different when you stand next to a single tree on the ground.

This book will help you see more clearly that, in each season of your life, God is indeed weaving His story into yours.

There are pages for notes to give you the opportunity to pause for reflection and to capture the thoughts you want to remember too.

I Found the Key

August 17, 2022

Jean! Can you hear me? Answer me, come on.

No answer.

Jean, I quietly whisper, I can't believe you're gone.

Jean, I have some of your traits

Jean, you're making your mark on the world.

Jean, I'm natural hair again and thirty years later,

deep pain pangs rush up from the bottom of my "belly bottom's" bottom,

in a moment's flashback to when you combed my plaits.

Remember?

Jean, I resisted talking about you. For many years I may not have been okay.

I guess I WAS okay.

As okay as I could, as I knew how.

I didn't realize that I was carrying a treasure

buried in my bosom.

Locked away.

Were you holding the key?

Dear Sister at the monastery, how did you know?

Who chose you for me?

Why did you invite me to come to talk?

I had nothing to say.

I had no words.

Remember?

Why did you ask if you could put your arms around me?

What were you thinking?

What did you see?

Your arms gently shifted my focus so that

I had to stare… into Jean's eyes.

Her closed eyes.

The lifeless eyes, closed for too long.

Shut tight.

My eyes resisted, I tried to look away.

My crumbling heart had no feet to stand, it gave way.

My brittle iced heart, melted.

Your arms became to me the hands of

The skilful Surgeon

Skilful Surgeon You took care to unravel my heart

With precision and the gentlest of care.

Touching only what needed to be touched

in the deep wound of thirty years.

Time stood still.

Time was patient.

It stood still, it waited

It waited long enough,

until I could hear my heart again.

I turned, I looked up, I looked across.

I look back and only after four years I realized

it was then that I found the key.

I found Jean.

CHAPTER ONE

Facing the Pain

I remember the day clearly one October afternoon in 2017. I was on the sofa sharing my heart with my husband Carey about my teenage years. I recalled an exchange between my father and one of my siblings. My memory took me back in time to the very moment. This time though, anger started bubbling up inside. It became so strong that I pelted off the sofa, paced the floor and continued expressing my anger and frustration as I re-lived the moment.

I grappled with my father's response and took the side of my sibling. On the face of it, it was a typical parent-child disagreement, but, given our family circumstances, I felt my father was being insensitive. Didn't he realize what my sibling could have been going through?

Still fuming inside, I went towards the phone intending to call him to talk about it. However, my husband, the calmer one in this moment, held me back gently and said, "Dear, I'm not really going to allow you to call your father in this state. You need to calm down first".

Carey was right. This incident happened over twenty years ago and clearly it still had a profound impact on me. Yet there was no way I could have a meaningful conversation or outcome by venting on my father, especially with no prior notice.

That same October, two missionary friends spent a few days at our home, and something came up during a dinner conversation that triggered pain in my heart again. That's when it dawned on me how much I had been suppressing my feelings of pain. My friends said I needed to let it out – that I needed to debrief.

Debrief? Was that necessary? That was so long ago! Should I really go back to visit that teenager.

Meet the Teenager

When I look back at my fifteen-year-old self, I see a young girl thrust into a new role overnight. As the eldest child, I found myself starting to take on responsibilities – parting fights, giving hugs to my siblings, helping with homework, sometimes taking care of my sister's grooming. My heart was shaping into a new role, one I did not feel prepared for. 'Am I supposed to be a mother or am I still a big sister?', I thought sometimes. I learned to be a Mo-Sister, a phrase I invented. My mother-heart was developing.

I quickly discovered journaling. To be honest, I just needed an outlet. Early mornings became a special time, yet at any time of day, you could find me pouring my heart into a notebook. Those books became the 'dumping ground' for my prayers, my feelings, the confusing and overwhelming thoughts. I wrote from my heart. It was my main escape.

Music was also my refuge. My father tells me that even from an early age, whenever he or my mother scolded me, they would soon hear the piano ringing through the house. Subconsciously, I found solace in music, although those earlier occasions have faded from my memory.

My father grieved openly during those years following my mother's death. I would hear him say, "I miss Jean", as he allowed the tears to flow. He expressed – he didn't hold in or hide his pain from us all the time. There was one thing he would tell me often: "Shaunelle, you need to cry. You need to let it out".

Yet, instead of following his example, I kept my emotions inside. The teenage me purposefully hid her pain. "I don't want to burden my father", she thought. Ridiculous as it seems, that was her logical thinking. So, my fifteen-year-old self didn't grieve with the support that she could have had. Instead, she bore her grief on paper.

My Journals gave a Clue

~

Sixteen years old

22 June. Lord Jesus, I fix my eyes on You now. Lord, I feel (though) cheated because I don't have a mother. I feel that it's just unfair to us, all four of us. I still see so many advantages in having her here.... You will never be taken away from me. So it's only You in whom I can put my trust. But I don't believe that You took her away so that You could just put someone else in her place. I believe that You must want to show us a new dimension of Your love that You can bring if we only

*allow You to. Lord, although I have acknowledged all of this,
please remind me constantly...God, keep reminding me that I
am Your child, and You are my Father.*

Twenty-three years old

*9 Feb. Today I saw a book my mother gave me when I was
young, helping children to understand death. The lady in the
story who died, her name is Auntie Jean.*

Twenty-seven years old

*March. Yesterday in "the family session" I released a lot of
anger. I cried a lot. I hurt a lot. I released my pain and
somehow, God touched me and healed my heart of pain I have
been carrying around... I am free. Free to be, in Christ. I still
have to discuss an issue with daddy but something inside me
has been unlocked. I am free and I am soaring to new heights.
The torrents of this last experience have lifted me higher.*

Thirty years old

*16 July. Lord, did it have to be this way? Did Mummy have to
die? Lord, if I had planned my life, I would have probably left
out all of what's happened in the last 4½ years. Honestly,
Lord. Couldn't You have found another way to draw me closer
to You? There's so much inner turmoil, I can hardly bear it.
I'm hurting so much, Lord, I don't know if I can deal with it. I
know that You can do many things, but I know You won't
bring Mummy back to life now. And that's what I want, a
relationship with my mother.*

Thirty-one years old

*9 May. Yesterday was Mother's Day, a day for me never to
forget. The day when I opened my heart to the Lord in an area
I've always kept from him...*

Six days later, 15 May. In functioning in my role as a big sister, I realize I find it hard because I internalise hurt that my siblings express. When they are unhappy about anything, I find that feelings of hurt build up inside me.

~

So, with all my journaling, was there more unexplored grief?

My journals also reflect that my grief was compounded by inner turmoil and pain, as I tried to accept that it was okay for my father to remarry. I was still trying to come to grips with Mummy's death and my new role as the teenage Mo-Sister. Thankfully, my father didn't wait on me to grieve before dating, otherwise he would still be unmarried!

In His love, God gave me a dream one ordinary summer morning while still a teenager living in Guyana. I awoke from the dream as my father entered the room to say goodbye before heading to work. Sleepily I told him about my mysterious dream of a newborn lying in a hospital crib. Tied onto the baby's tiny foot was a white card with a date. My father's jaw dropped when I told him the date. It matched Linda's birthdate – the woman who would eventually become my stepmother. That dream was to become a compass on my journey toward accepting another woman into our family.

I started connecting the dots. My journals carry the weight of years of my agony and pain mixed with pockets of relief. Yet I had hidden my grief from the world, and (as I was to realize later), in some ways, even from myself. Yet it was clear that my heart couldn't carry it anymore. This time, I needed something else than just more journaling.

I eventually phoned my father. He has been an anchor and a rock throughout the seasons of our lives. I shared about my anger that afternoon. I told him that it hurt. He listened keenly before sharing that he didn't know much about the world of therapy, nor did he think about counselling at that time. He told me that he was sorry that I was carrying the pain and explained that he did the best he knew how, to be a father to his four children who lost their mother suddenly.

I appreciated that Daddy listened. I held on to his parting words. He said, "Shaunelle, I can't go back to the past. All I can offer is that you go before God, pour out your pain to Him and allow Him to give you a song, or a word, or to respond to your heart in His own way."

So yes, I needed to debrief!

CHAPTER TWO

Retreating to Silence

One day during a conversation with a friend, I learned about a place to which people could go for personal retreats. I explored and discovered *Grandchamp* – a monastic community in the canton of Neuchâtel. Their invitation was to *"Come Away. Seek God's face, let Him draw near to you in solitude and silence, and make you whole by His love!"*[1]. It was only an hour's drive from my home.

Something stirred inside as soon as I walked onto the premises of Grandchamp on January 5, 2018. I held back the tears.

The monastery assigns one 'contact Sister' to each guest to explain how things work at the Community, and to draw alongside them if needed. My contact Sister[2] showed me

---

[1] www.grandchamp.org

[2] For the benefit of anonymity, I refer to the one assigned to me as 'Sister' or 'my Sister' throughout the book.

around, explaining things to me in a soft tone, in keeping with the quiet atmosphere.

It was a silent retreat – no talking to anyone – instead, you spend time communing with your Heavenly Father, while in community. When walking through the courtyard and in the shared spaces, you acknowledge those around you through nods and smiles, yet each person has the confidence to go through their personal journey without interruption.

Two things struck me. The first was that the community even ate meals in silence, except on Sunday after lunch. I had never experienced something like that before. My introverted side embraced that! The second thing was that they met three to four times a day in the chapel to pray, to sing and read scriptures and to sit together in silence. My Sister said that taking part in the chapel time was optional, yet those times were to become like a warm blanket around my aching heart. There was also a separate chapel dedicated to silent prayer to which I could go at any time.

She showed me to my room. It was quite simple. A single bed, a desk and chair with a red candle and matches, a welcome book, and a wash basin. I didn't need more than that. I noticed that the rooms had names. Mine was *Consolation*.

I was going to be there for four days – four days of quiet, no internet, no contact with the outside world – just me and my thoughts, my journal, and my Bible in an accepting community. Phone off and thrown in the bag, I looked forward to 'the disconnect'.

As Sister showed me around, I mentioned to her that I felt something stirring inside. I felt the stinging tears starting to well up under my eyelids. She told me that it was the Holy Spirit working in my heart. I tried to suppress my emotions, as usual, yet the tears burst through and hardly stopped for the four days that I spent there.

I did not realize at the time that God had been preparing me for 'heart surgery' and that the anger I felt back in October was only a symptom that a deep wound needed healing. The monastery was to be the operating theatre for the process of removing the 'abscess', and cleaning through layers of years of suppressed pain.

My Heavenly Father met me at the monastery.

When Sister saw the continuous tears, she invited me into a space to sit and share. I was hesitant, very hesitant. My tears had no words. What would I say?

I went in and sat with her in silence for a while, not knowing where to start really. My mind went right back to those teenage years. The intense pain came bubbling up and as I had learnt to do, I started suppressing the painful emotions. This time though, I started to let someone into my heart-space and into my pain.

She gently and sensitively encouraged me not to shut down. With my permission, she drew her chair closer to mine as I allowed myself to be in touch with my emotions. My body was getting limp as the weight of the pain overtook me.

Back to the Dreaded Moment

It started when I heard my dad call out, "Jean, Jean".

It was about five o'clock in the morning.

That night I slept on a mattress on the floor in the room next to my parents'. Our family was in the middle of a relocation, and we were preparing the furniture for shipment. It wasn't my room. In fact, I can't remember why I chose to sleep in that room that night.

I went over to their room to see my dad standing at the side of the bed, making several attempts to get Mummy to respond. He called her name over and over.

He tried mouth to mouth resuscitation. The air returned through her mouth. She wasn't responding.

He called a family friend and doctor who came over.

A short while after, my dad scooped up Mummy in his arms and they drove her to the hospital. It was before the break of day. I watched and waited, and watched and waited, for his return.

Later that morning Daddy returned from the hospital. He walked in and told me to get the others ready to go to the hospital.

"How is she?", I asked.

My dad looked at me as if trying to come to terms with the words that would need to leave his lips.

"Jean is dead!?!"

Those moments, on the morning of Wednesday, November 30, 1988, changed my life forever. I was the eldest of four children, the youngest barely six years old, and we were in the middle of our relocation from Jamaica to Guyana. It was also a big school exam year for me, and we were moving because of my father's work. We had already postponed the trip because my paternal grandfather had become sick. He later passed on. Daddy buried his father on Saturday and now, four days later his wife died unexpectedly.

Many questions filled my teenage years as I tried to come to terms with the new realities.

Our family eventually moved just over a month after my mother's death, where we started a new school, a new life, a new season. It was surreal.

Just three years before, when I was around twelve years old, there was a moment when I consciously put my faith in Jesus Christ, and I had been learning how to live out my faith as a teenager. Now, grief would be my companion.

In a sense, the faith I had started to grow since then, helped prepare me for life after my mother's death. My journaling took off. From the outside, it looked like everything was fine. And yes, a lot of things were going well – I did well in my exams, found favour with my teachers, joined the choir, started playing piano for my new school and held leadership positions. I continued piano classes and other extracurricular activities.

At home I became more involved in my siblings' world – helping with homework, parting fights, giving hugs; and when my dad travelled for work, even though we had household help, I was just being more of 'Mo-Sister'. I got involved in the choir at my church and played the piano there too.

My journals tell how much I drew strength from the Scriptures. I soaked up promises in the Bible to help me get through, especially those parts that reminded me that I was not alone, that God was with me.

I wrote my prayers, a lot of them, and there were many precious moments and dreams when it was as if God spoke directly to my fragile heart. I heard comforting words amidst the pain.

~

Twenty years old

Depression is like a dark road. My soul is dark, empty, emotionless, yet filled with unexpressed emotions. Sorrowful, anguished, in turmoil. I desire to see no light but just to cover up under the sheets and wallow...I don't feel like talking, like facing the world.

...Light flickers and having expressed myself I'm feeling normal again, a bit OK. I guess expressing does work. Do I do it every time? The headache is less. Thank You, Lord. Please give me the strength to endure today... help me to reach out to others, give me sensitivity. You are still worthy Lord, even if I don't shout it out all the time. I do appreciate Your undergirding. I have not fallen yet. You've always kept me up, regardless of how low I go.

Facing the Fear

Now, decades later in the room with Sister, it was as if the Holy Spirit Himself was beside me, giving me strength to bear the pain and face the fear. I had been afraid of being alone in my pain. I was not alone.

We sifted through my painful memories together. It was during those fragile moments that I unravelled the root of the fears I have lived with – the fear of being a burden to others, and the fear of being alone.

This was the turning point to a new season of discovery and healing. I found a key that changed the trajectory of certain recurring patterns of thinking and behaviour. When I pulled away to disconnect, it was a way to give God space to enter my heart, walk through my memories with me and to start a new phase of healing and wholeness.

What was the reason for this unravelling? And why did I carry the pain of all those years? Was there a bigger purpose for this pain and would I ever find out?

~

Looking back, I see it now.
My Heavenly Father was weaving His love story into mine.
I needed that away time at the monastery. The thing is, I
hadn't realized that was what I needed. And while pain was
my companion, God was with me.

You've Never Let Me Down

Twenty-four years old

The year began

I began to fly up

out of the valley of despair and depression.

With freedom, nothing holding me back.

The Lord had set me free.

You shall go out with joy.

And be led forth in peace.

The mountains and the hills will break forth before you into singing.

And all the trees of the field will clap their hands.[3]

With an exuberance like never before I was soaring.

Soaring into new things, fulfilled, enjoying life.

And I still am.

For life is to be lived in its fullness.

The fuller because of the challenges.

Fuller because of the winds.

---

[3] From Isaiah 55:12

Because of the rain,

Because of the stones.

The stones sometimes blister my feet

as they are now.

But though I trip,

I am not utterly cast down.

For lo I see it.

Yes, I see the hands of the One walking beside me.

I see His nail-scarred hands.

Love, warmth, care,

gentleness, strength,

power.

I see His hands reaching over.

And I stretch mine out to meet His.

I firmly grip His hand.

That familiar hand that had lifted me up before.

My hand is swallowed up in strength and I am secure.

He hasn't left. My best friend is still alongside me.

And he smiles with me, encourages me, and tells me he loves
me.

He is my company, my companion, my friend.

And I walk on.

Still slightly limping.

But holding on tighter than before, when I had slipped.

~

CHAPTER THREE

Unravelling the Layers

I left the monastery as a different person. I had gone back in time to November 30, 1988, and faced the pain of my mother's death. This time I was acutely aware that God was there with me. I felt His comfort – it was surreal. As I returned to the present, this reality gave me a new strength. Yet I knew that healing would be a process, not an overnight success story.

My heart was still very 'raw'. I was vulnerable. When I cried it was like pain-bursts from the deepest part of my being; so deep that, often, I didn't even make any sound. Pangs of pain came spontaneously, then it would go away, and I would move on and continue whatever I was doing.

"Lord, all I know is that stuff is happening inside. Please give me strength to stay in the place of healing."

I searched for music online to help cushion the pain pangs. I searched and listened, searched and listened. Could it really be that difficult? Even with a lot of music out there, I found that nothing satisfied, nothing connected with me.

It was an awkward season. Was there nothing to help soothe this aching heart that was committed not to suppress the pain?

Treating the Wound

A few days after returning from the monastery, I went to the doctor to treat a painful abscess that seemed to have developed. The doctor did minor surgery to remove it and gave me clear instructions: "I will leave the wound open and you need to wash it with pure water every day."

I was surprised that he said to leave the wound open. He said I needed to stay home for a couple of days to treat it, then return for him to check it before returning to work.

It was during this time while lying on the bed, propped up on the pillow, that I felt a strong impression, as if someone was writing a message on my heart. It was firm, yet gentle. I grabbed my journal to capture the message bubbling up.

~

In the same way that you have been under surgery for this infected abscess, I had to clean out the wound from the pain of your mother's death. You have had it inside, like poison, and I am doing surgery on your heart. The work started at the monastery. It has been painful, yet as you are washing the open wound with pure water day by day, so I am washing your wound. Each time you cry, I am washing you. And I am with you. It will be painful, but you must stay the course.

The impact of the pain is such that it colours your relationships, your view of the world. And so, when I am finished, you will be different; you will emerge whole, healed and ready to take on the new things I am bringing to you.

Trust me, stay the course. I have made provision for you.

My provision is there, and I love you.

~

I was too close to the situation to have made that analogy on my own and so I received this as a message from God.

I cried every day for many weeks, having made a vow to myself not to hold back the tears anymore – no more suppressing! I was so grateful for my husband, Carey, and his understanding heart during my journey.

An Outpour of Music into my Pain

This path was new; very, very new. I had already experienced the miracle of being able to return to very painful memories and I had made that vow not to suppress the tears. Something had shifted inside. Yet the pain pangs came at unpredictable times. There was work, normal home life and things to do. How was I to stay on the healing journey while living my regular life? This was much harder than I thought.

I sought out music again. My search for 'the right' music was futile and still nothing really resonated.

One day I sat at the piano and allowed my fingers to move across the keys. Slowly, softly, gently. I started playing songs I already knew, alternating with spontaneous bursts of improvised melodies. Before this, I rarely tried to compose songs without a purpose or occasion.

Strangely, I started to realize that something special was happening. I continued playing. My heart had a smile. Wait, did I find it? Did I find the music I was searching for?

I noticed that my aching heart was in a different place. It's as if God was giving me the music I needed to heal my raw heart.

Yes! I had found it! This was just what I needed. Yaaaaay! Hallelujah! My search was over! I started recording this music, over time, to accompany my pain. I played it in the background both at home and when I was out.

It was the beginning of a new era. My relationship to music was changing. This music touched me deeply and was weaving its way through my pain, bringing comfort to my heart.

My journal gives a clue:

~

July 11, 2018

Today I listened to music that I recorded during some quiet moments last week.

I don't remember exactly what was happening when I was playing then. What I know is that now, as I listened, I was drawn into a place of quietness and being still.

It was only 4 minutes 57 seconds of stillness, yet closing my eyes and allowing the music to transport me to a peaceful place inside was so precious. It touched a chord and I felt thankful – grateful for the gift God gives – Music.

~

Looking back, I see it now.
My Heavenly Father was weaving His love story into mine.
This music came straight from heaven's heart, to cradle mine.
I did not realize then, that He wanted to show me what it was like to walk with Him through pain. He was teaching me that, though pain was my companion, He too was with me. The One I am playing for understands – He formed my heart and knows it well.

CHAPTER FOUR

Post-surgery Check-ins

I booked time at the monastery a second time. I needed to pull away and be still for my Heavenly Father to continue doing work on my heart. I didn't know what to expect, yet I knew I was not alone. Coincidentally, it was forty days after the first visit.

I wrote my prayers in my journal:

~

My phone is now switched off. I have disconnected digitally. Now Lord, please do the work on my heart. I lay it before You. I feel a bit afraid, yet I know You are with me. Help me to stay with You:

To be present, with You in my mind

To NOT pull away when I feel pain

To receive the love that You give me

To hear Your word to me

~

Little Girl Alive

When I look back at this prayer, what jumps out at me was that I prayed that I would receive the love of God. Why? I look back at my journals and find that, through the years, this is my recurring prayer. Had I been resisting His love?

In the quiet moments over the days at the monastery, patterns of behaviour started coming to my mind. For example, I would often pull back (in my heart) when I started getting close to friends. Or sometimes I would want to reach out to connect with people but think that I'm bothering them. There are more observations too personal to write here, yet I was beginning to connect some dots.

When Sister and I sat together the first time, I made the painful visit to my teenage self. The teenager was embalmed and buried in lost memories. By God's grace, I went through the process of removing those layers. As I removed them, I saw something that I would never have noticed if I hadn't visited and taken time to be with her.

The teenager was still alive. She wanted someone to talk to. She wanted attention. She was the eldest child and had transitioned into a new role very quickly. When mother-figures came to visit the family home in Guyana, she put her siblings first and encouraged them to spend time with these ladies, because they did not have a mother. Yet deep down, how she longed for that attention herself – for them to sit with her, to be with her, to listen to her silent cries.

God provided mature ladies who lived in Guyana that gave her attention during those years. Two of them would spend time on the phone keeping her company and encouraging her. That was a longing fulfilled, to a great measure.

I also remember the attention and outpour of love from my aunts, uncles and other family and friends in Jamaica who were supportive to our grieving family.

When my father remarried, my dear stepmother gave me room to express, or be silent. She encouraged us to have Mummy's pictures up at home. We also shared tears, long chats and hugs throughout the journey.

All these gestures were like a warm hug around my heart, yet the inner turmoil continued.

Give her Something to Eat

On this same visit to the monastery, I read a story in the Bible that was instrumental in teaching me how to move forward in my journey of healing.

There was a leader named Jairus whose twelve-year-old daughter was sick. He went to the man called Jesus for help, yet while Jesus was on the way, someone from Jairus's house came and told him that his daughter had died and that he wasn't to bother him anymore. Jesus went with him to his house anyway, even though He had been busy with the needs of other people.

When they got to the house, Jesus sent the mourners outside and went to the place where the daughter was lying. He only allowed the girl's parents and three of His disciples to go into the room with Him. He took her by the hand and said,

"Talitha, cumi", which is translated, "Little girl, I say to you, arise"… and she got up at once and started walking around. When this happened, they were completely amazed. But Jesus gave them strict orders not to tell anyone, and He told them to give her something to eat. (Mark 5:42-43)

Give her something to eat. There was something significant about this statement. What was it, and what did this mean for me?

The meaning started to become clear as I shared it with Sister. I needed to pay attention to the teenage Shaunelle. I needed to listen to what she was feeling. It was important to start listening to her feelings of not wanting to be alone and to assure her that it was okay to want company. She needed someone to spend time with her when she felt fragile.

I had to learn to nourish and pay attention to her, something that I wasn't familiar with. More importantly, I needed to bring Jesus to her. This felt new, very new.

Back at the room I lay in silence. A song came to mind spontaneously.

In Your presence that's where I am strong
In Your presence O Lord my God
In Your presence that's where I belong
Seeking Your face
Touching Your grace
In the cleft of the Rock
In Your presence O God

(Integrity's Hosanna Music; Paul Wilbur)

The visits to the monastery became a part of my routine. I found that taking time to disconnect brought insight. It's as if the pulling away from my regular routine gave my Heavenly Father a chance to spend time with me in a different kind of way. I felt too that he delighted in revealing what was deep in my heart, and to heal me.

On another occasion, it happened again. I arrived and the tears started during the midday prayers. I hadn't been there for long, and this time I didn't really understand the tears; however, I knew better than to question what was happening. I knew my Father was doing His thing.

Pain pangs kept coming, both when I was alone and in the prayer times at chapel. As it turned out there were still emotions from the teenager I needed to acknowledge. Somehow, she needed acknowledgement for the care and emotional responsibility that she had taken on at that time.

Living through this process was tough. How was I to live with the things that were missing in my teenage years? I needed to accept that this was a journey. Although I was making progress, I felt it was slow and I needed to be patient with myself. How long would it take though?

CHAPTER FIVE

Finally Connecting the Dots

It was in my early twenties that I think I started the grieving process. Having left the family in Guyana to return to Jamaica for university, it really hit me that my mother was not alive. I had the opportunity to visit her grave on my own, as 'an adult' and was suddenly faced with the reality of her death in a way that I hadn't expected. It seemed as if, subconsciously, I believed that Mummy was still in Jamaica, since we had moved to Guyana so soon after her passing. Had I buried the pain?

I fooled myself in my teenage years and into adulthood, that I should not burden people with my pain. In my times of mourning, I felt I had to hide it, because no one would be able to change anything. I felt that I could only be consoled if my mother came back to life. Since that was impossible, I never believed I could ever be truly comforted.

Now that I have experienced comfort, I know that my thinking was flawed. I didn't understand the grieving process. I didn't realise that comfort is something that you receive over and over again, and that it was okay to feel pain.

~

Twenty-three years old

I must remind myself that the grieving process is ongoing. In grieving, understanding that Mummy is happy where she is, that God does things in His infinite wisdom… It doesn't mean that I can't miss her anymore.

~

Cutting Away the Dry Roots

Sometime after one of the monastery visits, I was taking one of my orchids to be watered, and it fell out of the pot accidentally. As an orchid lover I was not happy with myself for not paying closer attention. I rummaged through to see if all was lost and, as I evaluated the damage, I started to notice something.

I saw that there were old, dry, and withered roots right next to firmer ones from which fresh roots were being formed. I got the scissors to get rid of the dry, aged roots and I was curious at what I saw beneath the surface. I realized I had to be so careful to avoid cutting what looked like old roots but in fact were solid and from which new roots were emerging. Do I get rid of the old roots too or just the dry ones?

This orchid accident gave me the opportunity to see those that I needed to cut away because they were dry and taking up space and not contributing to the health of the orchid. I also saw the fresh new roots on which future beautiful flowers would be depending.

I confess that navigating an orchid's root system is not my area of expertise and, honestly, there was not a lot at stake if I made a bad cut, it was 'just' an orchid. Yet soon after, I saw immediate parallels to what was happening in my journey.

The outburst of anger, when talking to Carey on the sofa that Saturday afternoon in October 2017, was a signal of something happening beneath the surface. The time away at the monastery gave me an opportunity to start to gather clues and to see what was really happening.

I noticed that going back from time to time to an environment of prayerful solitude, reinforced by rhythms of quiet and stillness, became a helpful cycle. In those quiet moments as I listened to my heart, I picked up more clues along the way that helped me understand some of my recurring thought and behavioural patterns.

I had to learn how to cut away untruths that I had believed and replace them with new thoughts. The weekly watering and occasional plant food were like the rhythms of quiet and stillness in between monastery visits. It was through these times with my Heavenly Father that He nurtured my soul and continued to heal my heart.

For example, when I feel vulnerable in my relationships, I need to shift my attention to Him and embrace His view of who I am. Over time, the little teenager was growing up because she was being fed and given what she needed.

A New Season being Born

I believe that my Heavenly Father has been helping me connect the dots through different people and random everyday situations, like the orchid accident.

I was developing a skill of recognizing clues from my emotions and discovering how to nurture my heart. A new season was being born, while old ways of thinking were being cut away – thoughts that were ineffective in a season of new growth. I was starting to appreciate and celebrate the untapped potential.

Something else was happening as well.

I continued to play the piano – it was my safe place. Further, in this season I was comforted only by this music. I couldn't explain why. My Heavenly Father was giving me the notes to play and was using the melodies and the process to bring His healing to my heart.

I wanted to be connected to the music, even after I got up from the piano, so I had started recording the songs to access it remotely. It became a part of my routine – while winding down for bed, on my commute and as my company at work. The music brought calm and was like a companion in my healing.

One day my husband said, "I think you should share this music with people. There is something special about it." I resisted – this un-edited piano music was meant to be just for me.

However, with some nervousness, I finally gave in to his prodding to make it public, sharing it first on a one-to-one basis then to a wider group of friends and family. The responses were encouraging, and I realized that even though I was still going through my pain, others found the music calming and helpful for meditation. I eventually set up a mailing list and webpage to manage the wider distribution of the music. Was this my Heavenly Father's timing to bring out something new – new gifts, and new ways to use existing gifts, not just for me but for others?

I couldn't keep this life lesson to myself!

~

January 13, 2019

Dear friends,

When I made my private music collection public a week ago, I had no idea the journey it would have set me on.

This week taught me 3 things:

1. The power of one

It took one person, my husband Carey, to share his vision and influence me (via his gentle prodding) to expose this music. I am grateful for his constant encouragement and for often having a vision one step ahead of me. There were 124 persons across about 16 countries who were touched by the music. Never underestimate the value of a single, simple act.

2. The power of encouragement

I have been personally encouraged by the individual messages I received over the past week and that folks took the time to share how they used the music. Each message has reinforced that I should continue using the gift of music. Your encouragement can help keep someone going and be a lifeline.

3. The beauty from pain

I had no idea that songs would have come out of the pain I experienced, let alone recording and sharing them with anyone. In fact, about two years ago, someone shared a picture with me of a pestle and mortar – used to crush spices to bring out the beautiful aromas. I wonder now if this musical journey is what that was all about?

Beauty can come from pain.

~

I also didn't realize at the time that there was still more heart work, and beauty, ahead!

~

Looking back, I see it now.
My Heavenly Father was weaving His love story into mine –
but not only mine…
It was also for those connected to me who were touched by the
music. He encouraged me through their individual messages.
The thing is, I didn't even realize how much I needed that
encouragement.

CHAPTER SIX

Courage

It was almost two years since I had undergone the heart surgery at the monastery. I felt the shifts in my heart. Rhythms of retreat, regular times at the piano and journaling were my safe places, and they carried me along the healing journey. My mailing list was my community and I received frequent messages of encouragement. So even though I didn't speak to them about my mother, in my heart I felt their support as I continued to share piano music and life nuggets with them.

The term *SitAWhile* formed in my heart and shaped into something tangible – creating a space to pull away from the noise, to be still and experience calm. It was a time to disconnect from the routine, to listen to your heart and to God. It was a time for soul rest. Music was just a vehicle.

The power of being still while in community was also something I had been experiencing at the retreats. Visitors to the monastery, like me, were going through their respective journeys, with an awareness that we were not alone. There was encouragement and strength in knowing that those around also valued the sacredness of silence. Daily chapel gatherings had periods of silent worship, syncopated by readings of the Scriptures and community prayer.

To be a Mouthpiece

One weekend at Grandchamp, in June 2019, brought an interesting twist to my path. A lady played her violin while the community sat in silence. The music lifted off the strings and filled the chapel, stirring our hearts. It brought comfort, life, hope, calm, assurance. It set the atmosphere for a deeper work in my heart. In those moments, something resonated deeply inside beyond the sound of the music.

What if I could help people pull away from their routine to experience the gift of silence, in community? I had experienced the deep work in my heart when I pulled away from the noise. Could I also use music to create a sacred space for others?

The thought worked its way up and down my heart and mind and found a home. I returned from the monastery and mustered the courage to follow up on an idea that had now been lodged in my heart. I sent a simple note to the persons who came to mind.

~

July 2, 2019

Dear friends,

A few weeks ago I felt a strong urge to create a space for people to come and be still, in silence, while I play the piano.

I'm going out on a limb here because I haven't done something like this before, yet I can't seem to shake off the idea.

This is what I expect it will look like:

- *I will open my home for around 5 persons to come over;*

- *I will play piano for you, for me, for us, in an hour of pause and of stillness;*

- *You can sit on the carpet on cushions, on the sofa or the balcony - as you wish;*

- *You may come and leave anytime during that hour as you wish;*

- *It will give each person time for individual silent reflection, while in community;*

- *Now the strange thing is that there would be no talking between us during that hour :-).*

My wish is that you will leave feeling restored and refreshed.

If this is something that you would like to share in, please let me know.

The first one will be on Saturday July 6 from 9:30 - 10:30.
And you may come from 9:15 to get settled.

In anticipation of a good thing,

Shaunelle

~

I knew I was being vulnerable to extend this invitation to others, even though I was still not fully over my grief. Yet after beautiful moments with five persons spread across my living room, each having their own moment of pause, I knew God was up to something. I didn't realize at the time though that this invitation was going to be the first of many to come.

Then in 2022, instead of returning to the monastery, I created a three-night retreat for myself at the end of the year at a hotel in the eastern part of Switzerland. It was at a hotel nestled in a perfect spot overlooking Lake Constance, next to two chapels – one even dated back to the year 779! It was such a profound and beautiful time that I stayed an extra unplanned night.

As I drank in the beauty of the surroundings during my last moments by the lake, I found myself speaking out my heart's desire. Lord, I want to run retreats – in-person retreats. It was spontaneous, yet I knew my desire came from a deep place. Since that first SitAWhile in my living room, and throughout the monthly SitAWhile sessions on Zoom, there had been a gentle bubbling of desire building up. In the twinkle of these moments, I decided that I was going to give in and live even more fully, from the inside out.

As the idea germinated, the thought of hosting a getaway weekend resonated strongly. It struck perfectly with the tuning fork that was emitting 'PURPOSE', and I did not hold back.

As I did in 2019, I returned home and prepared invitations for a retreat to be held at the same hotel. I didn't wait till everything was figured out before sending them to the persons that came to my heart, albeit nervously.

When the first person that registered was from the UK, I believe that was God's way of telling me, 'You're not going to talk yourself out of this; stay the course, keep going, purpose is calling and there's something special ahead.'

As I was preparing to deliver the retreat, I felt a shift in the invitation. This was actually a deeper call from God to us, to come away to be with Him – an invitation to create space and time for Him even beyond this retreat I was planning. I felt the weight of the responsibility to make this a request to respond, not to my invitation but to His call – a call to carve out space for deep communion with Him, and to pursue His rest.

My Heavenly Father had touched my heart in such a profound way that I just wanted to share one message with the world – *Take time to pause, to pull away with your Heavenly Father.*

The in-person SitAWhile retreat concept was born – a place for leaders and those often in 'giving mode', to pull away from their routine, to rest and nurture their souls.

With the gift of the Grandchamp experience in my heart, I designed the retreat with flexibility and simplicity so each person could have their personal rhythm and space to rest.

Was my journey through layers of healing now becoming an instrument in my Heavenly Father's hand, to touch others too? Time will tell, however there was something that I hadn't had the courage to do before – share openly about Mummy in our community of family and friends.

Remembering Jean Harris

My last verbal conversation with Mummy is still fresh in my mind. I came home from school on the afternoon of Tuesday November 29, 1988, and reminded her about prizegiving the following day. "Mummy, are you going to come?" "Shaunelle, you know I can't come without bringing something to do while waiting. I may have to take something with me to hem", she said with a chuckle. My mother was a high school teacher of the subjects mathematics and computer studies[4]. She also sewed for people and still had orders to complete before leaving for Guyana. I wasn't sure whether she was joking and planned to come anyway, or not. She passed on early the following morning.

She was in her early forties and lived a full life. She was always involved in people's lives, helping in phenomenal ways, even while raising her four children. Those she left behind wonder how she did it. She made me a part of her

---

[4] She introduced this subject into the curriculum of the school

story, taking me around with her when she did things for others.

She often spoke of her death though. Did she know?

My mother walked briskly, spoke quickly and got a lot of things done. Yet I would see her sitting down to have a quiet moment with a cup of tea. Not multitasking, just sipping. Then she would get up and go again. This memory reminds me of a rhythm I've found helpful in busy seasons – the power of short bursts of pause for physical and soul rest.

She would sometimes get up during the night to take advantage of the quietness while getting things done. In her own way, she found rhythms of pause and solitude.

My father also planted a seed of rest in my mind because, as a child, he would often say, "I'm going to take a five". After lying across the bed with his eyes closed for five to ten minutes, he would get up, re-energized, a daily habit that has continued to this day.

I wanted some more information on what my mother was really like though. I needed to fill some gaps, not just for me but for my younger family members who didn't have the privilege of having her around.

At the time of writing this memoir, my mother would have been close to eighty years old. When a child loses a parent at an early age, with time the memories of specific interactions fade, with no possibility of refreshing them as they grow into adulthood. In a real sense, we (continue to) live the memories of our mother through stories from those who knew her.

In 2020 as the anniversary of Mummy's death came around, I took a bold step to have a SitAWhile in her honour – sharing memories, interspersed by piano music. Back in 2018 I had sent an email to friends and family to ask them to share their memories of her with us. I wrote a note to explain that I had started the journey of trying to capture the memories that are fading with age. I told them I was capturing them not just for me, but for my siblings and my nieces and nephews, to paint a picture of someone who has been so significant in our lives. They hadn't had an opportunity to meet her.

I had no idea where the journey would take us as a family, but I shared that, '*One of the things I have learnt is that there are some outcomes that are worth the long and sometimes painful journey.*' I sensed that this was one of them.

The invitation went out to join our family for a special edition of SitAWhile – *Remembering Jean Harris*. It played a significant role in our lives and not just in ours. Some participants expressed that this helped them bring them 'closure' since our family left Jamaica so soon after she died. The community of friends and family finally had a chance to pay their respects and bond with us as a family.

That event was a treasure for the family and the timing was also important because two key people who held memories of my mother, passed on in a few short months afterwards.

It was also a milestone in my journey, not just because of the new memories I was forming, it was the courage for us all to spend a full weekend talking about our mother together. It was refreshing to finally experience this, in community.

The recording of that weekend will be a treasure for the younger ones in our family, in years to come.

~

Jean E. Harris

Jean lives on in our hearts as Mummy, Sister, Auntie, Cousin, Teacher, friend and simply, Jean!

Community: Not Merely One

July 2024

A part of my community

you think you're just

another

Your smile, your words

the silent nods,

my sister and my brother

you are to me

You don't grasp how

your presence cheers me on

Be yourself, and stay in touch,

you are

not merely one

~

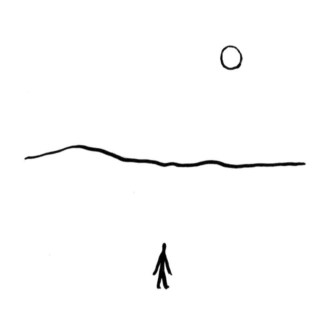

CHAPTER SEVEN

Finding your Rhythm

Whitney Houston's song: *I Will Always Love You,* has a pregnant pause that takes the song to a whole new level. *Selah* is a musical term in the Hebrew Bible, known to signal a time to pause, or to stop and consider. Taking a pause on a hectic day is like a marathoner who stops by the water station for a few short seconds to help her/him keep going. A two- or three-week family vacation can help refresh family bonds and reset the mind before the return to work. *Our rhythms of rest have a profound and direct impact on our capacity to bring our best selves to the world, sustainably.*

There are many motivations for taking timeout, or better yet, to build a routine infused by timeouts of various sorts. Some people have daily or weekly rhythms, for others, their annual vacation, long weekends and occasional retreats are fitting opportunities to reset and recharge.

The first four-day silent retreat in 2018 was a turning point in my life. It was four days of an unhurried, un-rushed pace, filled with space to flow without a strict agenda. It was a precious gift of time in a quiet atmosphere and a chance to listen to my heart, and to my Heavenly Father.

It was listening time.

To Listen

Many people would agree that active listening is an essential life skill, though not as widely mastered. What is less often acknowledged is the significance of listening to your heart—paying attention to your emotions and the feelings that lie beneath the surface.

Life-changes that evoke negative emotions can lead to unfavourable patterns of behaviour; for instance, recurring immature conduct in relationships, or anger expressed disproportionately. They may be ways of masking underlying grief, pain or unresolved issues.

I wonder how many teenagers – grief-stricken over death, a family breakup or relocation – are grappling with emotions that need a healthy place to be expressed? How many adults, successful by the world's standards, or who show recurring unhelpful behaviour, are living with a grieving teenager inside? The pain lodged in their young hearts, is neatly tucked away from the world and perhaps, even from themselves. Beneath layers of learning how to function very well, they hide behind their success, albeit relying on emotional crutches.

Do you listen to your heart sometimes? Taking time to really listen to your heart involves paying attention to the emotions beneath the initial ones – the vulnerable feelings, the longings, the unspoken fears – and noticing the thoughts that trigger them.

Do you sometimes feel the need for unhurried alone time to 'sort out' your thoughts? This could be your body sending a message that you need to take timeout, or a nudge from your Heavenly Father to pull away for alone time.

Creating space for unhurried alone time is crucial. Whether it's to listen to your thoughts, connect with God, or simply let out pent-up emotions, that solitude becomes a sanctuary. However, being still can be difficult, let alone listening to your heart.

I'd be fidgeting too much. I can't sit still.
My schedule doesn't allow it
I wouldn't know what to do
There's too much to do
I can't do that
Waste of time
Scary
No time
It's boring
I don't want to hear my thoughts
My family situation doesn't allow it
Stillness is not for me; I must keep moving
If this is a meditation thing, I do that already

If you can identify with any of these, you are not alone. As much as I am a strong advocate for being still to listen to my heart and to make time for solitude, the reality is that, if I don't bake it in intentionally, 'life' overthrows my good intentions.

> *The screen sucks me in, but I can't help myself*
> *I find it hard to spend time with God*
> *I'm just trying to find peace*
> *I'm often anxious*
> *I feel burnt out*
> *I need calm*
> *I'm overworked*
> *I sleep but I don't rest*
> *I just need peace of mind*
> *Honestly, I know I should slow down but...*
> *I feel like I'm always too busy, I know I need to change*

Building unhurried routines is like the baby steps of a toddler starting to walk. It's bumpy at first. The toddler falls, holds on and, with practice, finally migrates to the liberating achievement of independence. Even with their new-found freedom, at times, they want their parents to lift them into the comfort of their arms.

What is assuring is that our Heavenly Father wants to share His heart with us, to reveal the secrets of His heart, and help us deal with the layers of 'stuff' that we may be carrying around.

As Jesus and his disciples were on their way, he came to a village where a woman named Martha opened her home to him. She had a sister **called Mary, who sat at the Lord's feet listening to what he said.** But Martha was distracted by all the preparations that had to be made. She came to him and asked, "Lord, don't you care that my sister has left me to do the work by myself? Tell her to help me!"

"Martha, Martha," the Lord answered, "you are worried and upset about many things, but few things are needed—or indeed only one. Mary has chosen what is better, and it will not be taken away from her."

(Luke 10:38; author's emphasis)

The Lord is my shepherd; I shall not want. He makes me to lie down in green pastures; He leads me beside the still waters. He restores my soul…

(Psalm 23:1-3; NKJV)

~

His Presence is enough

Yes it is enough

Selah

His love is kind

Yes He is love

Selah

(Extract from the poem *Selah Is Your Love*, Shaunelle Harris Drake.)

~

When you confide in a friend, their attention sharpens. They set aside distractions and lean in to listen. You share intimate moments in soft tones and an ambiance of trust. Unravelling delicate emotions of your heart with God often happens in the hush of quiet and stillness. So too, pulling away to have special time to share your heart with Him is fitting.

But have you found that sometimes there are just no words to express the depth of your emotions? Or you have no clue how to describe your feelings?

Sometimes your emotions can feel as bland as water. This too is normal, and it's easy to fall for the stillness-activity trap – to set aside time to be still, then distract yourself, or fill the time with activity. Or you may be tempted to obsess with getting it right, or to make it a ritual, full of form and devoid of meaning. The goal is simply to respond to that deeper call from your Heavenly Father to come aside and be with Him, then let Him direct your heart.

Sanctuary

July 2024

A secret shared with one who stops to listen

has value like diamond and makes the heart glisten

I lean in, listen fully with all my heart

Heavenly Father now I wait, gently do Your part

~

Over the years I've bumped into different practices that help carry me along the time set aside to listen to my heart.

Below are six practices that help to express the sentiments of my heart. *They have become words* that continue to bring insight, and a channel of God's healing power. They are especially helpful when I can't find words on my own.

I can never predict what the experience will yield – not that I must account for the time spent – yet often, I feel a shift inside my heart. And when my deeper emotions bubble up, I am learning to lay them before Him one by one.

1. [5]*Playing piano*: Listening with my fingers and in my heart for a melody as I sit at the piano. I play the first notes, then follow every note in faith without knowing if, in the end, it will have a pleasing sound. I play on anyway, till the melody and song end.

2. *Finding images*: Listening with my eyes, scanning other people's drawings and/or images, until something resonates within my heart. Sometimes I go further to produce an amateur representation of an image, tracing the contours slowly with my eyes till it becomes my own expression.

3. *Choosing colours*: Listening with my eyes and heart as they seek out hues that capture the emotions of my story. Sometimes, I search for a colour that symbolizes my feelings or a profound thought. When I find it, I choose the colour from my crayons to create something very personal to my heart.

4. *Writing words*: Listening is penning sentences and words without the burden of seeking validation from an

---

[5] Most of the music at www.sitawhile.org comes from this.

audience. I write my prayers, and wishes, my raw emotions, the ordinary, the extra ordinary, words, sentences, prose, poetry... whatever flows from within. And when there are no more words, the pen stops.

5. *Reading words*: Listening, I immerse myself in the narratives of others, and find the words and phrases that echo my own emotion. I weave their expressions into my own, grateful too that I am not alone. Listening here includes audio. I also return to read my writings of the past, weeks, months and years.

6. *Silence*: Listening is telling myself to stop, and to surrender to the silence. I allow it to envelope my emotions. I may simply close my eyes in a quiet place, or listen to water by a lake, go for a silent walk or sit in the wee hours of the morning. I let the silence speak on my behalf.

~

These practices are helpful in helping me listen, and to be aware when layers of emotion may be building up. However, there's sometimes a tug of war and restlessness in my heart when I try to control how to spend the time or analyse my emotions too much. Then frustrated, I remind myself that it's not my duty to figure it all out – this is the work of the Holy Spirit. He knows when to reveal what's happening beneath the surface and when I need to simply trust that He is taking care of it. It is indeed a journey to learn to simply listen, follow the promptings and experience Him in this way.

What could help you listen to your heart, and give space to healthy expressions of your emotions? In an unhurried way, consider experimenting with different tools to find your heart's words, and God's heartbeat. Ironically, the key to unlocking your own words, is to listen. *You are unique.* Let His heart beat against yours, and instruct you.

Remembering to Remember

In the pages of this book, I share the role of stillness and being quiet in my healing. Yet it's the practice of journaling that made it possible to pen this book – as I scoured years of written dreams, pain and unanswered questions, all the way back to my teenage years.

Journaling helps us remember. Though there are pages of my journal that I want to forget, like a scar from a wound that I cannot erase, they tell me a story. It is God's story of love in my story, now his-story and a testimony of His grace.

My memory could not hold the record of the journey, and journaling on paper is one way I make sure to remember. However, I've discovered several other enjoyable journaling practices to help me remember the journey. These include filling my daily gratitude book, capturing moments through photographs, making video and audio diaries, drawing and colouring, to name a few.

What is your way of remembering?

~

Looking back, I see it now.
My Heavenly Father was weaving His love story into mine.
He infused His creativity to give me words to express the pain,
and heal my heart... and He hasn't stopped!

Panting

December 2023

This is not art

It is my heart

It's the hart panting

after streams of water

It's my soul panting

Wanting to be anchored

in something secure, unshakeable

Wait what is this

Beckoning

Come over here

and sip this

Slowly slowly

Then take a long drink

Oh man, I can't do slow,

I have to run

I will come back

But no I can't go

I must do slow

My soul cannot bear

another day

of not being

of not living

from the inside out

with no anchor

living less-than

Then feeling purpose-less

Wait

Wait my soul

You must stay

Wait

Try

I looked

I stooped

Yes I stooped down to drink

To drink it in

To P A U S E and

do S L O W

do S T I L L

To B R E A T H E

IN OUT IN OUT IN OUT IN OUT

To listen to my heart

To try to listen to God

Tears streaming

Heart healing

Burdens lifting

Doing S T I L L

B E I NG still

B E I N G

Did I find it

did I actually find it?

Yes, I found it

I found it!

Stillness you are here

I found Y O U

And my soul hears

In the quiet I hear it clearly

It's not by my will that

I succeed

Not how high I jump

nor how fast I run

nor how strong I am

It is the sheer

grace and mercy

of G O D

Soul did you hear well?

Drink it in

Fill-up my soul

Anchor in it

And be free

And now you can go!

Today jump and run

and be strong or be weak

Just my soul, please

please be free

and find your rest

in God alone

As the deer pants for streams of water, so my soul pants for you, my God. My soul thirsts for God, for the living God. When can I go and meet with God?

(Psalm 42:1-2)

~

Dear Reader,

What would it take for you to respond fully to His call to pull away to be with Him, as a part of the rhythm of your life?

Be still. Listen.

Wait…

Be still. Listen.

What is your heart saying?

I invite you to pause for a moment and tell Him.

Shaunelle

CHAPTER EIGHT

The Last Conversation

Over the years, my dreams have played a significant role in speaking to issues in my heart, and relationships. The real last conversation with my mother was in a dream.

In the dream, I was transported up a hillside, lush green surroundings. There was a sense of everything being perfect and serene. As I was ascending, I saw that my mother was there ahead of me. I was delighted to see her; however, there was a light that took my attention away from her. As I drew closer, I noticed something unfamiliar and difficult to capture fully.

This very bright light was transmitting an emotion. It was the most beautiful emotion I had ever felt, and it swallowed up any other emotion in that moment. It was a love emotion that engulfed me. It was magnetic. My attempt to describe the experience is feeble in comparison with the reality of the warm and inviting pull of the love light towards it.

I was delighted that I was going towards both the light and my mother. I was revelling in the warmth of the emotion when something started to block me from going any further. My heart reached out as if trying to resist the gentle power that stopped me. My mother, in closer proximity to the light, was also being drawn towards it. Our eyes met. My heart said to her, "I want to stay with you".

She looked toward the light, looked back at me, then looked away and became pre-occupied with the light which was greater and stronger. I slowly started to drift back down the hillside as she was drawn to the light.

That last conversation was only with our eyes. I was sad. I could not stay with her. However, my sadness turns to comfort and a smile even comes to my face when I relive the taste of my experience with the light. She was going to be living in that love experience, all the time. This is my confidence and assurance.

For I am convinced that neither death nor life, neither angels nor demons, neither the present nor the future, nor any powers, neither height nor depth, nor anything else in all creation, will be able to separate us from the love of God that is in Christ Jesus our Lord.

(Romans 8:38-39)

~

Looking back, I see it now.
My Heavenly Father had woven His precious love story into
mine.
He has turned my ashes into beauty and He wants you to
grasp the depth of His love story in your story too.

Epilogue

Dealing with pent up and conflicting emotions, as a firstborn with unprocessed grief, pain and sadness layered with typical teenage hormonal changes, loyalty to my mother, happiness for my father's remarriage, transitioning from sister to Mo-Sister and back to sister, was not a walk in the park!

The teenage me purposefully hid her pain because I didn't know how to do otherwise. Thankfully, by the grace of God, journaling, being involved in many (music-based) activities, counselling in my twenties, a supportive extended family structure and very good friendships, my emotions found healthy ways to be expressed.

But is it better to let sleeping dogs lie? Maybe. The dogs didn't give notice though, when thirty years later, a deep-seated anger reared its head out of the blue. The connection to my mother was not obvious.

A scar is a symbol of both pain and healing, and this journey shows that it is possible to truly heal from buried pain and disappointment. This is a story of heart surgery thirty years later, to pull out the sting of the pain, and how the recovery journey led to new rhythms that had a greater impact than I could ever imagine. This is God's story of love, in my story.

Weaving in regular times to be still may mean intentionally placing it in your calendar (with a reminder) to practice and to experiment while being patient with yourself along the way.

Routines around pause and stillness can help you to recover, recharge, rejuvenate, relax, restore, realign and rest. There is no one-size-fits-all approach to finding your rhythm. In a quiet moment as you listen to your heart, reflect on what could be helpful to you.

Pulling away to be with God is a gift and a treasure, and experiencing its benefits is a journey, a pursuit even. Whatever that journey looks like in practical terms is between you and Him.

My wish for you is that you find healthy ways to express your emotions, and that you have courage to pay attention to the emotions beneath the emotions. My strong encouragement is that you find ways to slow down enough to listen to your heart, and to your Creator and Heavenly Father.

Listening in Colour

In this section I gift you with one of the newer creative practices that have helped me face my own emotions – *choosing colours*. This can be a relaxing, creative activity at any time, though the true intent is to help you slow down your thoughts and have a refreshing time with your Heavenly Father. There is no obligation to use the guidelines below, do what works for you.

What do you need?

~ First, make an appointment with yourself, aiming for at least ten minutes. I suggest putting it in your agenda.

~ Select a location, ideally a quiet place where you will be free to express emotions outwardly, if needed.

~ Crayons, faith and (optionally) a journal or something to write on.

Prepare to colour

~ Take a few deep breaths to help slow down your breathing. Be present.

~ Pray: *My Creator and Heavenly Father, please open my heart to You in these quiet moments. I dedicate this time to listening to You.* (It may help to write down this prayer and/or pray it slowly.)

~ Go to the page of the colouring text and, first, simply let your eyes scan through the text a few times, not necessarily reading deeply. Then when you are ready, pause to read the text more intentionally, in your mind or out loud, as you prefer.

~ When a word or phrase jumps out at you, stop. Stay present right there.

~ Close your eyes and keep that word in your mind. Visualise it, with your eyes closed. Pray: *Why did that word/phrase jump out at me?* Be still and be conscious of any feelings or thoughts.

~ If you were to put a colour or colours to the image, word or phrase, what would it be?

~ There is no right or wrong colour because this is deeply personal.

SitAWhile Colouring [6]

~ Select the crayon that matches the colour you just associated with the image/word and start colouring it. Colour slowly. Be intentional. There is no rush. Do not let any 'art rules' constrain your colouring or distract you. If colours go outside the line, it's ok.

~ Flow in the moment. You may use empty spaces to doodle images or shapes and any jottings that come to mind suddenly 'from nowhere'.

~ Pause to write thoughts that come and go, or do it at the end. Stop whenever you feel it's time to stop.

---

[6] Contact me at sitawhile.org to request a printable colouring PDF.

Wind down, Close out.

~ Lay the paper down. Look at your colouring. Take it in. Then close your eyes, take a deep breath and visualise it. This will help to keep what is important to you, deep in your heart.

~ Pray: *Thank You Father for being with me in these quiet moments. Thank You for speaking, and I trust You to continue to speak into my heart as I leave this space. Keep me in Your peace. Amen!*

~ Write your initials and the date on the page. Take a deep breath and return to your routine. Plan for another one as needed.

~

Dear reader, please feel free to explore *listening in colour,* using the following reflection texts, in a way that suits you.

EVEN IF PAIN
IS MY
COMPANION,
GOD IS WITH ME.
HIS PRESENCE
IS AN
EXPRESSION
OF HIS LOVE.

UNPLUG
PAUSE REST
STILL
TIME OUT BREATHE
PRAY
RETREAT
SILENCE

THE GOD
OF ALL
COMFORT
COMFORTS
US IN ALL
OUR
TROUBLES

Solitude, rest and stillness

The Lord is my shepherd; I shall not want. He makes me to lie down in green pastures; He leads me beside the still waters. He restores my soul... (Psalm 23:1-3; NKJV)

Whoever dwells in the shelter of the Most High will rest in the shadow of the Almighty. I will say of the LORD, "He is my refuge and my fortress, my God, in whom I trust." (Psalm 91:1-2)

Come to me, all you who are weary and burdened, and I will give you rest. Take my yoke upon you and learn from me, for I am gentle and humble in heart, and you will find rest for your souls. For my yoke is easy and my burden is light. (Matthew 11:28-30)

Immediately Jesus made the disciples get into the boat and go on ahead of him to the other side, while he dismissed the crowd. After he had dismissed them, he went up on a mountainside by himself to pray. Later that night, he was there alone. (Matthew 14:22-23)

Compassion for those who mourn

As he (Jesus) approached the town gate, a dead person was being carried out—the only son of his mother, and she was a widow. And a large crowd from the town was with her. When the Lord saw her, his heart went out to her and he said, "Don't cry." Then he went up and touched the bier they were carrying him on, and the bearers stood still. He said, "Young man, I say to you, get up!" The dead man sat up and began to talk, and Jesus gave him back to his mother. (Luke 7:12-15)

Praise be to the God and Father of our Lord Jesus Christ, the Father of compassion and the God of all comfort, who comforts us in all our troubles, so that we can comfort those in any trouble with the comfort we ourselves receive from God. (2 Corinthians 1:3-4)

Don't do life alone

Two are better than one, Because they have a good reward for their labour. For if they fall, one will lift up his companion. But woe to him who is alone when he falls, For he has no one to help him up. Again, if two lie down together, they will keep warm; But how can one be warm alone? Though one may be over-powered by another, two can withstand him. And a threefold cord is not quickly broken. (Ecclesiastes 4:9-12; NKJV)

Acknowledgements

This book would have remained handwritten notes in my journals, an unfinished work on my computer or a dream, if it were not for: Katya Lodge, Marie Lavis and David Lee Martin.

Katya, you raised your hand to let me know that if ever I needed someone to do the editing, you were available. I knew I could entrust this sensitive story to your hands and heart. Thank you for your dedication and love. As a dear friend I deeply appreciate very much your outpouring of love into this work as if it was your own.

I'd been waiting for the right time to do a creative collaboration with Marie, so she was the first person I asked to be the illustrator. Over the years, I witnessed her diligence in taking time to get in the mind of her clients and, with sensitivity, craft pieces of art that seem perfect. Marie, your illustrations bring the text to life beyond what I could ask for, and I appreciate you.

David launched his *90-days-to-published* programme for first time authors at a time when I was suffering from 'writers' loneliness', and my aspiration of daily writing for ten to twenty minutes needed accountability. *Anointed Authors* was the community of like-minded individuals that made it possible for me. David has been a coach extraordinaire, shepherding, encouraging and teasing God's gifts out of us.

Thank you Ros, Tim, Lori, Gemima, Barbara, Margie, Ana and the rest of the cohort for standing with me so that my first draft could have been completed within 90 days. David, your giftings played a key role in bringing out all our books!

My dear husband Carey, special thanks for being my sounding board during critical sections of the book, and for holding my hand as I grieved. You have a sensitive and understanding heart that wows me every time. Special thanks for accommodating the disruption to our weekly Thursday routine during the 90 days with the Anointed Authors group. I appreciate you.

After I wrote the first draft, I remembered that Aryana Roberts told me, "If you ever do any writing, I would be happy to read or help in anyway." As a writer and fellow silent retreater at Grandchamp, I knew she would value the perspectives of retreat and healing. Thank you for being the other pair of eyes to help tease out important bits in the story and the overall work. You encouraged me, and God knew you were to be a part of this too.

My family – my permanent community that cheers me on in my (sometimes very wild) projects. Thank you, Daddy, for filling me in with key facts to complement my fading memory. Thank you, Linda, for not trying to take my mother's place, and for the space to grieve. You all have been my safe space on the journey, and I don't take for granted how blessed I am, to be free to be me with you all.

The time I spent at the Community of Grandchamp has been a lifesaver and I express my deep appreciation for the sisters in this monastic community who faithfully serve. They continue to open their community to those that come for a place to be still and to rest. This is the community that welcomes me every time I need to pull away from my routine to experience silence and solitude. I have no words to express my deepest gratitude to God and His Holy Spirit for how He accompanied me on this journey.

It takes a community to live out your gifts fully. Alongside my family and family friends, my SitAWhile mailing list and monthly *SitAWhiler's* have been like family along the journey. Even though I didn't always speak about my mother, in my heart I felt your support as I continued to share piano music and life nuggets from my journey. Thank you for staying.

To everyone who has been part of this journey, your support and love have made this book possible. Thank you.

About the Author

Playing the piano, journaling and praying have been a part of Shaunelle's life since she was a child and when she lost her mother at the age of fifteen, she drew strength from these. She discovered the power of stillness and silence in her healing journey from the pain of that loss, only decades later.

Shaunelle has held various professional roles in the airline sector. She believes that our skills, life experiences and an intentional mindset, help to pull us forward into our purpose and positively affect the world. The world needs our passion and gifts, sustained by rhythms of rest and retreat.

Since 2019, she hosts monthly group SitAWhile hours of pause for those who want to be intentional about regularly creating a space to be still, and has run online, day and weekend retreats.

She comes from a close-knit Christian family and has lived in Switzerland, Canada, Guyana, the UK and her home country,

Jamaica. She is married to her best friend, Carey Drake, and is the eldest of five children.

Connect with Shaunelle and her music at sitawhile.org or send her a voice note at speakpipe.com/shaunelle.

Notes and Reflections

Notes and Reflections

Made in the USA
Columbia, SC
29 October 2024

44858135R00061